JOY COME FORTH!

JOY COME FORTH!

the resurrection of j.c.

j.c. Crawford

Joy Come Forth!

Copyright © 2000 – 2007 James L. Crawford

All rights reserved

No part of this book may be reproduced by any mechanical, photographic or electronic process, or in the form of a phonographic recording, nor may it be stored in a retrieval system, transmitted or otherwise be copied for public or private use- other than "fair use" without written permission of the publisher.

ISBN: 978-0-6151-6549-3

DEDICATION

This book is dedicated to my children.
James, Derik, Ciara, Kendrick, Kelsea and
Jacob. Also to my Grandchildren; Evan Dean &
Audrey Renee Crawford.

May God Bless you, as only a True Father can.
If this book be my legacy…
Let it be for thee.

I Love You

Dad

Acknowledgements

A simple thank you seems so minuscule of a gesture to offer all of the people that gave freely of their time, talent and love. And before I mention any one person in particular; I want to thank every person that has touched my life since birth. It's like dad spanking everybody just to make sure he didn't miss anybody. Truly, I believe that every person that you touch, will leave a little of themselves with you. I pray that I left good stuff when I touched you all.
Thank you.

To James Crawford Jr. and Bonnita K. Shears; my parents, Thank you for "training" and not just raising me. For giving me a solid rock as a foundation, my heart is anchored to you. I praise God for the resurrection and restoration of our families. Rosalie thank you for your undying faith and support, especially when times were dark.

To Pastor Keith Reynolds for being "My Main Man", the dynamics of our relationship have been the source of understanding to me that cannot be understood unless you know me. PK you know me. You always have a way of making me move. You are more than a pastor or mentor. You are a great friend. I love you bro. But, I will never go to the gym with you again.

To Bernice King you know I'm hard headed, so don't sit there with your mouth wide open. Your diligence and patience and putting up with, and sometimes laughing at my stupid jokes, puts you high on my list. Your timely reference to Psalms 119 changed the way I looked at this whole project profoundly. What more could you ask from a friend?

To the man who learned to hug me, and his wife who one can't help but hug; Wayne and Betty Feay. When I hear phrases like; *Heart and Soul* or *Lion and the Lamb* or

Abbot and Costello, I can't help but think of you. Your Love and compassion made your home feel like a little piece of Heaven.

To all of my "20 Something's": Lisa Reyes, Abby, Shauna, Paige, Christy, Don, Ramon, Josh, Kay, Becca, Rachel, Trish and all the rest of the Goldfish / Cupcake / Seekers/Fellowship crew. You guys make an old man feel young, sometimes it hurt my body. I will miss Monday Nights. To my Remedy youth and volunteers that have been my psuedo-kids and family from my very first day. The "Love Monster" is a reality thanks to you all. Look out for the J and J sammich. Love you John Smoot. Thank you Jeff and Kathy Dotson, Susan, Diane, Becky, and Ben, Phil, Loren and Nick (your getting old).

To my Kinfolk, Shana, Eathan, Gordy (I meant to do that) Nate and Candi. No matter how far or how old you get…I'm still the Oldest and the best looking. You can't win this one cause it's my book.

Thank you Nini for letting me have your room. Shawn, stop trippin. KiKi, lift the seat!

A special thank you to Pastor Dave Deselm; I could never tire of your teaching. Your vision is amazing and your willingness to be vulnerable has truly blessed me. Exodus4: 2 changed my life. The day God asked me that question: "what is in your hand?" the answer was an ink pen and a pad, that day I started writing again. Thank you for listening to God's voice. You are a true shepherd.

To all those who think I should have put your name in here… X_____

There's your blank. I still love you, but you must remember that I am getting older and more forgetful by the second.

Finally To my Heavenly Father; I thank You for this breath, and now that one, for an eternity. I pray Lord that I may decrease, so that You may increase. May You put this token of my expression where You see fit. Thank You for Your Word, and Your Spirit that You pour so freely into my heart to the point of overflowing. In the words of my mentor… Lord I L.O.V.E You!

Jc

CONTENTS:

Dedication

Acknowledgements

Introduction

BOOK ONE

BIBLICAL INSPIRATIONS

- ~ Abide
- ~ Good Advice
- ~ Joy Come Forth
- ~ Read the Signs
- ~ Royalty
- ~ Thought for Today

BOOK TWO

WRITINGS ON THE WALL

- ~ A Clever Card *(I Love You…)*
- ~ All About You
- ~ I Said Merry
- ~ I'm a What?
- ~ J.E.S.U.S / C.H.R.I.S.T
- ~ Open the Door
- ~ The Incredible Shrinking God
- ~ W' man
- ~ You Do What is Right

BOOK THREE

FROM THE REMEDY *(Inspired by FMC Student Life Ministry)*

- ~ Feb. 17, 2006
- ~ Free? Yes You
- ~ Hang in There Baby
- ~ Jan. 4, Prayer
- ~ My Usual Day
- ~ Ode to a Friend *(Pastor Keith's Poem)*
- ~ The Game
- ~ Three Monkeys Ditty
- ~ W.W.J.D.?

BOOK FOUR

I PLAY THE DRUMS… I AINT' GOT NO MELODY

- ~ Chopstix (sung to the tune of Chopsticks duh!)
- ~ Every Day *Erin's Song*
- ~ Praise The Lord!
- ~ That Crazy Man
- ~ The Sequel
- ~ Until You

"An Ode to the Mothers" Followed by a note and reflection section.

Introduction

"My son, my son how many times do we have to go over this?" The father was not angry, just frustrated. He had hoped his son would have learned this lesson by now.

His son once again, was finding himself in trouble as a result of making the same old decisions without regard to the consequences. "Father, I am so sorry, I try so hard and then something I can't even explain makes me do the stupid things I do. Even when I know they are wrong. And the thing that makes me feel even worse, is knowing that when I do finally get caught, or feel so bad that I have to tell you, I know you will always forgive me and try to help me through my problem, Always."

This sounds like an excerpt from some sad after school special. It could well be, but for some who read this, it could be your own personal conversation with your Heavenly Father. I know it's mine. It is considerably sad to know that some of us share the "prodigal disease", which makes us run away, then run back, just to run away again. Never thinking that there may come a time that running back may not be an option.

And just like in the excerpt above; God graciously takes us back, cleans us up, and then rejoices in us coming to our senses.

Simply put; there is absolutely nothing, nothing at all that God cannot over- come.

There is nothing that God cannot forgive. God already knew what you did, have done, and is about to do. The problem we have is that He also gives us freedom of choice. That freedom, compounded by our instinctively self-serving nature, usually leads to bad decisions or just down right disobedience.

So, if you are anything like me, you have probably read every book on our nature, or repentance or the "prodigal disease". And you're wondering what I' am going to say different…Nothing. That's right; I'm not even going to pretend to know enough on the subject to help anyone.

What I do know, and the purpose of this book is; God has brought me through so much stuff. He has allowed me to live for myself and survive. And now, years after my final welcome back party, I'm living and writing for Him. Giving Him all honor and glory for all that He has done in my life.

The name of the book represents what I lost and then found in Christ: Joy… the unspeakable, unashamed and sometimes unbridled type of joy. Joy in knowing that I am clean, saved and forgiven by the Blood of Jesus. He died so that I may live in Joy Land.

The writings that follow are a result of that resurrection within me. Just like Lazarus; I was dead, stinky and in the dark cave. Thanks to Jesus I can choose Joy.

Read, think and reflect. Choose life…Choose to let your Joy Come Forth.

jc

BOOK ONE

Biblical Inspirations

Before Jesus even spoke the words to Satan after His fasting in the wilderness. God had made known to His people, that although He may lead them to a sometimes-painful understanding of Him, that He would never forsake them. Our only source should be our faith and His word. As He did then, He can and still does provide for us today in ways that we could never imagine. (Deut 8: 3)

For me, God's word is my main source of hope and inspiration, joy and consolation, chastisement and encouragement. I can go there when I feel there is nothing else, and there is where God shows up. My writing process is to feel it, write it, and then research it in the Bible, to keep what I write contemporary but with a solid scriptural foundation.

My prayer is that as you read these pages, you take the time to search for the foundation of each piece and then see if God shows up for you…

He Always Does….Joy Come Forth!
jc

Abide
John 15: 4-7 (NLT)

Abide with us Oh Spirit, and from us do not depart…
Comfort us Oh Spirit…come bless our broken hearts.

Abide with us Dear Savior; We need to feel You here
Come stay with us Sweet Jesus…and save us from our fear.

At times we are so lonely, and we push Your love away…
Your Spirit and Mercy falls on us and guides us on our way

Come speak to us Our Father… We lift our praise to You
We call Your name, you hear our voices calling out to You

Abide with us Holy Spirit; quicken our spirits now
Set aflame our souls within, as only You know how

Sometimes we want to praise You, and our words they seem so small
Come speak for us Oh Spirit, when to God our spirits call.

Keep us near Jehovah, whether our numbers are large or few
And by Your grace we pray oh God, let us abide in You.

By jc

Good Advice
Proverbs 20: 5-7 (NLT)

In this wonderful world we live in
It's often very nice…
To know that when we need it most
We can always find advice.

Ask for it? No need to…
It will come before you ask…
But before you take that advice to heart
Be sure it meets your task.

Some parents like to give advice
As you're walking out the door…
Usually that's good advice,
Cause where you're going…they've been there before.

Advice sometimes comes from a very close friend
With a hug when your life has you down…
And it's usually because you didn't listen the first time
But your friend is still around.

Now you can get advice from anywhere,
From tapes and mags and books…
Advice on how to become rich,
And why you need to change your looks.

Some advice you get for free
But that doesn't mean no cost

Cause following someone's bad advice
Can surely leave you lost.

In the book of Proverbs, read it yourself
God has something to say:
"The Godly give good advice to their friends,
The wicked leads them astray.

So here's my advice…don't look so surprised,
You know I had to do it
Seek Godly counsel, from Godly people,
Then, seek God if you should do it.

By jc

Joy Come Forth!
John 11: 41-44 (KJV)

It makes me weep…
Just to think of the love that Jesus has for me.
I sometimes have to look beyond the cross…
To see Him as not just my savior,
But also as a man—just like me.

Feeling love…just like me
Feeling pain …just like me
Feeling the full gambit of emotions, that makes Him just like me.

The hardest thing to handle is, He Is God!
And God came down to my level to be just like me.
To teach me, to live like me
To be the ultimate example of what Just like Me should be.

Who could have done better?
Who but Christ could be God and be ridiculed by His own people?
Who but Christ could heal the sick, raise the dead and still be doubted.
I am humbled by His ability to love and forgive beyond the circumstances…
Who but God could pray for the people nailing Him to the cross?

Today, just as then, I feel Jesus is crying out for our benefit…
"Father forgive them for they know not what they do!"
Jesus' eternal prayer… for our Never changing world.
And we still
Don't know what we do…

Moving so fast that we realize often way too late…
We have separated ourselves from the one who came before, and is here now to rescue us.
And God's still small voice keeps saying…
"Be still and know that I am God" Peace Be Still…
Hey World! I am here! Look, I am that I am!

As for me, I am full…
My cup runs over with joy!
Because of God's grace, I have one more chance to say
Thank You Jesus!
Thank you, for standing in front of my tomb and crying…
Joy come forth!
My son, rise up from your walking death, and live in Me.
My joy is your salvation…
Joy Come Forth! What problem do you have that I can't overcome?
Joy Come Forth! What have you done so badly that I, God cannot forgive?
Joy Come Forth! Stand up my child and Live!

By jc

Read The Signs
Matt 25:37-40 (NLT)

Take the time to read the signs of those we meet and greet each day...
The signs that tell what's in the heart... which they'll never say.
The Lady that comes to the church each day, and sits there all alone...
The sign she wears says "VACANCY" and here is better than home.

The man with the kids at the grocery store, who's one "daddy can I?" away from crying...
His signs says "LOST & WHY ME GOD?" Cause his wife is at home and dying.
How about "that girl" you know the one, she lives just up the street...
You read her sign hooker but it really says, "HELP", my kids have no food to eat.

My sign says "GUILTY" and "JUDGE" and "DESENSATIZED" and it may be your sign too...
We move so fast that we forget the things that Jesus asked us to do.
Why should we stop and read their signs? We have signs of our own...
Sometimes it's "sick" or " hungry" or naked...
Or sometimes "I just feel all alone"

So hear what it says...it's written in red. It's what Jesus says you see...
"What so ever you do for the least of these My brothers and sisters,
You have done also for Me".
Jesus says visit, Jesus says heal, Jesus says feed the hungry and poor.
The "sign of the Times" says walk on by... What sign are you looking for?
By jc

Royalty
II Corinthians 6:17,18 (NLT)

We are children of The King.
We are His sons and daughters
We are princes and princesses
Royal children of the Father...

Tell me how can we look forward to living in castles,
When we offer ourselves to the streets?
Tell me how do we share in the Kings Victory
When we live where we know there's defeat?

Look at yourself My Son, dear prince,
Do you seek God in everything?
Or is your desire to serve your flesh?
Is sex your worldly King?

My princess my princess, Daughter of God
What lies ahead for you?
Save yourself for a prince from God
Your King would want that for you.

We are children of The King.
We are His sons and daughters
We are princes and princesses
Royal children of the Father...

To honor our King in purity,
is truly a great sacrifice.
Be true to yourself; be true to your King
Be pure like the Prince Jesus Christ.

By jc

THOUGHT FOR TODAY
Proverbs 3: 27(NLT) & 1 John 4: 18(NLT)

Have you ever been just chilling' just doing what you do…
Walk right past a homeless person, then they say "God bless you?"

Did you not see the sign? Or did you just see the filth?
Did his God bless you statement just slam your heart with guilt?

Did your heart suddenly stop you? Did your eyes start to tear?
Did you not turn around, paralyzed by your fear?

Perfect love casts out fear…not fearfully passes love by.
What if Jesus threw His hands up, when God asked Him to die?
Did you judge this poor beggar, simply by the way that you think?
"He's not begging for food" you say to yourself, "he'll just go buy a drink".

Now don't think that I'm judging, cause I've done this before;
I bought the man a burger…so how could he want any more?

Oh yes he ate it and thanked me… trust me I waited for that.
Then he told me one burger wouldn't make his 4 kids fat.

So I write this for me and all people the same.
In particular those whom claim Jesus' name

Don't hang on to your treasures… don't walk by unaware…
You may be one tragedy from sleeping under the stairs.

By jc

BOOK TWO

Writings On The Wall

I wish that I could say that *everything* that I've written was "inspired by God". Technically that would be true, but in fact there are so many people, places and events that move me into the "writing zone".

Things such as: My desire to write cards for the "Crown People", rude people who don't have a clue about what Christmas is really all about, and if I could have told her how I really feel...sorry, I digress. *"Open the Door"* was inspired by a homecoming, delayed by almost thirty years of pride.

I am also inspired, as many are, buy the teachings, and insights of my beloved pastor. Dave Deselm is one of God's truly anointed. *"You do what is right"* and *"Open the Door"* are both poems inspired by Dave's teaching.* To me, Dave is the Captain Kirk of pastors, His mission: To boldly go where no church has gone before. Fellowship Missionary Church is proof positive that God is alive and well in South Fort Wayne, Indiana. In Dave's own words..."The gates of hell shall not stand against it"; which is a mission of motion... but that's a different sermon.

Sometimes, God just moves me; I write and then leave it alone, all the time knowing that there will be some time or some place where someone will hear the call... Joy Come Forth!

jc

A Clever Card

What you're holding in your hand is more than just a card…
It's a subtle way of saying something, which I'm finding very hard.
The thing I need to tell you, I think you already know.
I just wish the guy who's writing this would hurry and let it go!

Every time I try to tell you this, my body starts to shiver
And I feel it every time we kiss, every time it makes me quiver.
It happened to my parents… and to your mom and dad…

OK! Mister poet guy… now I'm getting really Mad!

I'm trying to say *I Love You*, but you keep writing stupid verses.
What do you mean go back a line!? I'm trying to say…oh curses.

Yeah Right, I Love You…and You knew it too, *But you bought the card…* What Ever!
You just got this card; cause you looked inside and saw the poet was so clever.
Like ok dude chill with the rhymes the point is made all right?
So both of us can part our ways, and I'll just say goodnight!

Note from writer
This idiot really does Love You
And they have great taste in cards!

By jc

All About You

I'm not drunk, and I haven't gone mad…
In fact, I'm dancing cause my soul is glad.

I am a total 360 from what I used to be…
And it's all because Jesus died for me.

Now I still can get discouraged, and life sometimes get me down…
But I realize it's only temporary, as I take a look around.

My life before Christ was leading me to death.
So now every morning I wake up, I praise Him for every breath.

I don't profess to be perfect, it's impossible for me…
But for the sake of those who watch me, I strive in futility.

Oh yes I know they're watching, saying, "watch the Christian fall"…
On the days I'm focused on Jesus, it doesn't bother me at all.

It's those other days; you know the ones…
When you're hungry, angry, lonely or tired that makes you want to run.

Sometimes I do run, sometimes I run so very far.
But if I stop and pray, I get the message…don't run! Jesus won the War!

What I'm fighting is a battle, against forces I cannot see.
My m.o.s. is Proclaimer, that through Christ proclaim victory.

So now, what you're hearing may seem to be about me, in fact that may be true.
But look down deep, check yourself, how much of this story is you?

You don't have to lose your battles either; you don't have to run so far
You can claim the Blood of Jesus, no matter who you are.

Following Christ is not easy, if fact sometimes it's tough...
But look at the life your living now, have you messed it up enough?
Are you sick of being tired, are you tired of feeling sick?
Are the words you're hearing at this moment, cutting to the quick?

Right now! You can be forgiven...
Right now! You can be free...
Right now! Jesus is waiting...He's a gentleman you see

Don't wait until tomorrow, to ask your Lord Jesus in...
Cause the moment that you ask Him, your new life can begin.

A life that proclaims victory over sin and guilt and shame
A life that changes all it's around, just by calling on His name...

And maybe someday someone will ask you
Are you drunk? Have you gone mad?!

Stop dancing for a second, wipe tears of joy from your eyes, and say...

No, I'm not drunk; No I haven't gone mad...
I dancing in the spirit of God, and He has made me Glad.

Then remember this poem, go dance some more, and realize as I do...
It really wasn't all about me...It was always all about you.

By jc

I Said Merry Christmas!!!!

I told you Merry Christmas...
Without guilt, or fear or shame.
Because the Lord Christ Jesus
is the reason for the name.
The first part "Christ", is for the Child,
who's birth we celebrate.
The second part "Mass" is for the multitudes
who celebrate the date.

Now allow me to elaborate,
on what it is I believe...
And if you find this offensive,
Then you my friend can leave.
Or better yet, just stick around,
and maybe you will see...
That the child who's birth we celebrate
Also died for you and me.

And for that reason, I won't "X" Him out
You believe what you want to believe.
By His birth and His death and His resurrection,
I've been given AUTHORITY
Authority and power to stand in His name,
against evil and man's tyranny
To NOT shrink in fear of saying His name
I'm a CHRISTIAN, it's expected of me.

So I give thee fair warning, and I challenge thee too
When thou getteth the feeling, just do what I do.

If I tell you Merry Christmas, and you act like you
didn't hear
I'll shout, "I said Merry Christ- Mass....and Happy
New Year!"
By jc

I'm A What?

You say what? I'm a new creation? Sometimes I ask myself How did that happen?
He lived sinless, He healed the sick, He was whipped, and spit on and died and buried.
He went down into the depths of hell and paid the price for my sins...MY SINS.
He rose up, Did ya catch that? ROSE up... Smellin sweet. From the dead. For What?
So that I could be a new Creation?

Oh yeah that's deep, so deep I'm gonna back it up a bit...I remember when my life wasn't worth the spit I spat trying to be somebody. I remember times when death would have been better than the life I had before me. I remember crying out...I WANT TO BE SOMETHING...TO SOMEBODY!

He Heard, I am.

And now this man, this God man, has taken me back beyond the womb. Beyond the First Creation and told me that because HE loves me...I can also be a Sweet Smelling Rose...Rising up through the filthy cracks of my past. Reformed, Reborn, Renewed by His Blood. A new Creation.

So now what? What do I do now that I am new? I do what Jesus did. Yeah, I will Bleed to save one. I will bare my cross with pain and honor. And now I can hear the cries, I can feel the pains, I can help the souls that cry out; I want to be something to somebody!!

Hello poor soul, I am a new creation...I know this man named Jesus... and you too can be a ROSE.

By jc

Jesus Christ

J ...is for *Judgment,* in last days of this earth. When the things you've done are set before God, since the moment of your birth.

E ... is for *Eternity,* the time your soul will dwell. The righteous spend it in heaven, the sinner will see hell.

S ... is for *Salvation,* Gods free gift to save the lost. His son paid the price; His son set us free, when He died upon the cross.

U ... is for *Unconditional,* it's the type of love God shared, when He offered salvation to One and All, as the cross of Christ was bared.

S ... is for our *Savior; H*is blood was shed to save. *JESUS* is the only way to Heaven from the grave.

How Can You Be Saved?

C ... Call on Jesus, confess your sins and ask to be forgiven.

H ... He will hear you, just ask Him in, and change the way you're living.

R ... Remember, that we All have sinned and fall short of the glory of God.

I ... Immediately, He will forgive your sins. That really means a lot.

S ... Search His Word, The Bible will help guide you.

T ... Tell a pastor, or a Christian friend, ask them to walk beside you.

By jc

Open The Door

They say you really don't know what you have until its gone...
With that I can partially agree.

But let me explain the feeling of loss, as it really pertains to me.

Some things you don't miss, cause you just give it away...
Just chucked it out, and turned around and then just walked away.

Now for some folks it's their faith in God, for some folk childhood
dreams.

And for some folks well they're just perfect, at least that's how it seems.

For me it was my family, I left behind one day. I left the house I flew the coupe
Man I was on my way.

I'd give a call every now and then just to let them know I was alive, and send a card at
the appropriate time...but would never make the drive.

Now don't start judging, my childhood wasn't bad, for the most part it was good, although
divorced, and not always right, my parents did what they could.

But I grew up thinking just like you did… "When I grow up I wont be like them".
But I did and I am, and what was worse I had the same name?

OK now to the door I eluded to, the one that I mentioned in the title.
It's the door to the heart, the heart that's in need of revival.

My door was a stone that was rolled in front, so hard nothing could get through
Now I know that when Jesus rolled His stone away. He rolled my stone away too.

He opened the door to forgiveness; He opened the door to heal.
All of the broken parts behind the door, that only He can heal.

I call on my God as ABBA. My Father in heaven and earth.
And now I call on my Daddy and Momma God loaned me to at birth.

Can you feel your heart beating? Or is that really a knock?
You may have some healing behind your door. Jesus has the key to the lock.

So here's a new saying, just as true as the saying before...
You can treasure the now times, and forgive what you missed,
Trust in Jesus and open the door.

By jc

The Incredible Shrinking God

My God is an awesome God…He reigns from heaven above…
That is one song that is so true.

But Sunday is now Monday, and you're back at the job
Tell me is this what some of us do?

Our God starts to shrink out of sight out of mind,
We fall into our worldly routine.

We talk and we act like the other folks do
And our God is nowhere to be seen

You catch yourself cursing and telling old jokes
And thinking things that are not right

Your lamp is now empty; it lays in the dark
And at work God put you as the light.

Ok that's just one-way to watch our God shrink
Now let me explain yet another

This is not meant to pass guilt or judge
These words are to encourage each other

We've all had our share of times that we feel
Like our problems are too large to bear

If our God was still Awesome, like he was Sunday morn
We'd rejoice knowing that he was there.

But nooo God starts shrinking; He's gotten so small,
That we worry and fret for tomorrow

We forget God supplies our every need,
And we sentence our selves to sorrow.

Sometimes it's so hard, and I know how you feel
I know cause I've been there myself

But when I read Gods word I soon realize, yet again
He's too big to fit on my shelf

God is the Omni of Omnis, He's in everything
That we do and that we see

So when I open my eyes I say How Great Thou Art
And give praise that God is Bigger than me.

By jc

W' man

Wo man... bone of my bones, flesh of my flesh, created by God for Man as a companion, a helper...praise be to God the Creator.

Wow man... Adam the first to behold God's 1st Wonder of the World, She in all of her glory shall become, The mother of all mankind, The tempted, The temptation,
The Mother of God's only son, and the reason Jesus wept.

Woe man... cause her not to worry, provide for her as a Man should, respect and
Honor her as if she is part of your flesh,

W/0 man... for this reason a Man shall leave his mother and father and cleave/ hold/cling/ not let go of his wife and they shall become one flesh...completed by each other not without.

Whoa Man... let not your anger fall upon this gift from God...Treat her tenderly,
With the grace and loving kindness that God has also shown Man.

Woman... after man, before man, of man and bore man. May God bless all women that they become all that He intends for them. Father instill in all men that all women are to be treated as your gift to us and to be loved honored and cherished.
Blessed be the man who is truly loved by a woman.

By jc

You Do What is Right

Although many toils and trial my come…
And your way may seem as dark as the night
Hold fast to your faith, hold on to your God…
My child you do what is right.

When it seems like this world has run so far ahead
And your spirit has lost the will to fight…
Remember His promise to never forsake you
Remember, you do what is right.

My sons you may be tempted, to fall and compromise
To go left instead of taking the right…
That one left turn will "kill your spirit"
My sons, you do what is right.

Oh my daughters, your virtue is precious
Not to be lost to a whisper in the night
Let the words of God's spirit; speak comfort to your soul.
My daughters, you do what is right.

I know it's not easy, to do the right thing…
When it seems all around you has taken flight.
But when you stand before God, take heart for he knows you…
As my child… the one that does what is right.

By jc

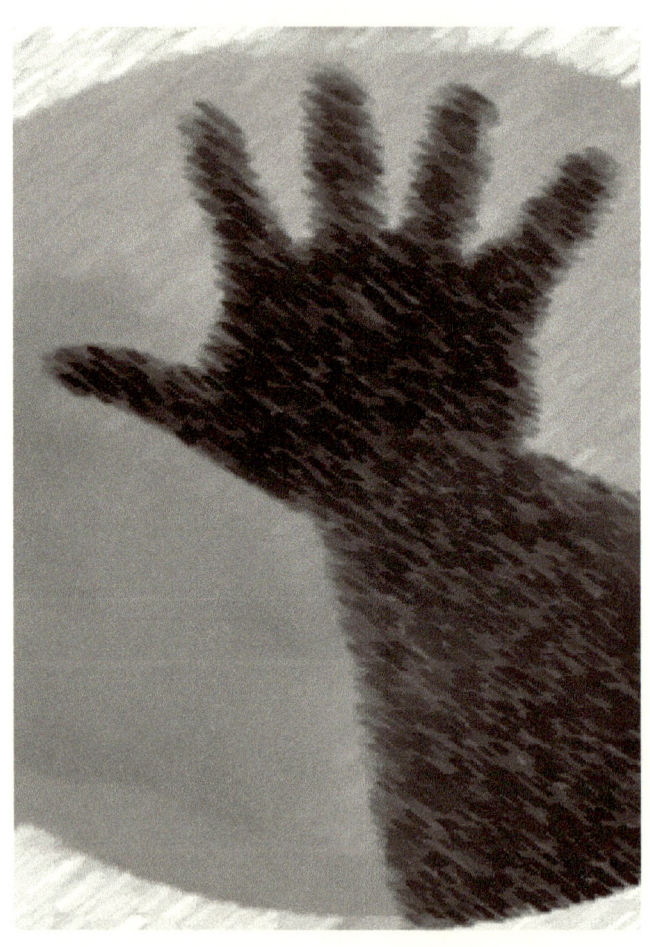

Abba Father, today I reach out my hand to you. Praying that you are out there reaching out to grab hold of me. Like a child who has lost hold of his father's grasp and fallen, Lord, lift me up and hold me close. Wipe away my tears, dust me off, kiss my boo-boos and set me back on track. I need you now. I love you.
Amen.

BOOK THREE

From "The Remedy"

Train up a child in the way he should go: and when he is old he shall not depart from it.
(Proverbs 22: 6)
To those of you involved in youth ministry, I applaud you, and pray God's grace upon your very souls; for *training* up a child is no easy task, a when those children are not your own it can get down right ugly! And if you have *been in* long enough, you get the biggest eye- opener of all…"It's not about you" or me, or what we like or what we are comfortable with. It is about them, the "kids". As cliché and scary as it may sound: they are the future of the church, and this nation.
Pastors Clinton Faupel, Keith Reynolds and Jim Deselm, spearhead the Student Life Ministry at FMC. Along with dozens of young adult and not so young adults (my group), they have provided a clear direction for coming along side our young people and showing them as much Jesus as we can muster. Like any position dealing with pre-teens and high school aged young people we also face the frustrations and disappointments that come with the calling.
So you ask, (maybe not) … jc what is it you do to bring yourself into the favor of the wild and wicked youth of today? My first response is RUN! Just kidding. One day after writing "Feb

17, 2006" I was searching for God in the bible and found;
I Corinthians 9:19-27. It said to me that I need to not just see, but sometime "be" a child, or Goth, or prep, or punk, or skater, or hip-hop dancer, or tech nerd just to plant a seed.
If you are ever so blessed to experience Student Life's REMEDY night, and you see a very large black dude head banging with a bunch of white kids: don't freak out! That would be me, getting my groove on and letting my...

Joy Come Forth!

jc

Feb. 17, 2006

The page is blank...well, not anymore I don't even know what I started writing for.

Tonight I think, tonight I wonder, Tonight I'll let my simple mind wander.

Why do I let my heart be affected? I thought I was safe, I thought I was protected

Why do I care, what these kids do...? Then Jesus said "it's not about you".

I always try to give the kids me, but it's Jesus that I want them to see.

They get me frustrated, and it makes me sad, and then at times it makes me mad

That as smart as they act, no matter how hard I've tried... They can't open up to let Christ inside.

They come in the church and play with my God, when I ask them to listen to hear what He's got.

But they laugh and they snicker like they don't understand. If they would just listen they might just hear the plan.

I know Lord, I know Lord, and it's not about me.

But if I don't show them how else will they see?

Thank you Lord for answers, you'd think by now I'd know.

All I can do is plant the seed, only You can make it grow.

Well I just wanted to tell You in my own special way, that I Love where You placed me, even after today

Forgive me for worry, and anger, and stress.
Forgive me for not always giving Your best.

I thank You for the kids, and for putting me here, and for Your grace to which I hold so dear.

By jc

FREE?

Yes you…

What part of free don't you understand?
Weighed down by the chains of your mind…
You've been set free; you're no longer a slave
What master are you trying to find?

The symbol of freedom is before you…
The Christ on the cross is the One
The power of the flesh is a strong one
But, its power over you is done.

You've cried to the Lord…please forgive me!
Now in faith believe that it's true
The blood of Jesus has opened your cell
Drop the shackles, and walk on through.

A rich man was told to sell all of your wealth;
To give it all up and follow Me…
You see, to get into heaven won't cost you a dime…
You can't charge it, or buy it, Its FREE!

From your sins…You Are Free!
By God's grace…You Are Free!
Jesus' stripes and death completed the task.
All you need to do, to receive your free gift…
Is to freely come to Jesus and ask.

By jc

Hang In There Baby

For all you babies, you know who you are…
The new on this journey, that haven't gone far.

You made a decision, the biggest of your life…
Bigger than the house, the car, or husband, or wife.

Try not to get discouraged, and don't stray too far…
Just hang in there baby, God knows who you are.

He will never hurt you, though some pain you will feel…
And all of your suffering, Only He can heal.

And no more guilt and no more shame, no living in the past…
Hang in there baby, Your sins ARE forgiven, and this time won't be the last.

There's gonna be times when you feel so alone…
Hang in there baby… God sits on the throne.

The journey is a long one; you won't do it in a day…
And the Bible gives direction, to help you along the way.

Now Baby is not a bad thing, in fact it's really good

Cause as a child, our Heavenly Father, will love you as only He could.

Keep taking steps and know right now, you'll stumble and sometimes fall
But get back up, Hang in there Baby, You'll make it through it all.

And there may come a time when things get so dark, and you won't know what to do…
Just think of Jesus, and then remember His Cross… He Hung on there for you

For God so Loved You Baby, That He Sacrificed His Son.
Jesus Hung in There Baby, so you and God could be one.

Remember Jesus came to us as a Baby, He did what had to be done.
And now the ONLY way to the Father, is By Hangin With the Son.

So Hang on in there baby, and I'll tell you one thing true…
Just when you think you lost your grip, You'll find God's Hangin on to you.

By jc

Jan 4 Pray

I am feeling a little lost these days; unable to answer my ever-questioning mind. Weary from tossing and turning, over things I have no business trying to carry on my shoulders…

Why Lord do You love me so much? So much that it leaves me, of all people…speechless. Lord I praise You for Your infinite mercy and for Your Grace… that sustains me.

Thank You Lord for Your gentle sweet voice. That like a whispering wind…envelops me, then tells me to let…it…go… Lay it all down…Exhale my child.

Peace is God… Joy is a gift He offers. Love is a commandment, strange that You have to command us to Love… Children follow the examples of their parents…why is it so hard to follow Your example?

I feel that wind again; I can hear the whisper… Don't forget one…
One what Lord?
One of Mine… Love them all. See them all…
As I saw you, remember?
Exhale…
I am the only true free gift. Give Me to them
Start, and don't forget one.

By jc

My Usual Day…

I woke up this morning, wanting to write a psalm of praise…
I walked out to my terrace to see the sunrise, like I usually start my days.

I heard the birds singing …the wind rustling through the trees…
I was listening for some inspiration, just a whisper from God you see?

I was trying hard to think of something, to begin my song of praise.
Then I remembered to read my Bible, like I usually start my days.

What words could I say, that would let my God know…
That I love Him and I need Him and I worship Him so?

Then it suddenly hit me, as it usually does…
There's no formula for worship, in fact there never was.

You wake up, You walk out, you listen and pray…
You worship and praise Him by giving Him your day.

I realize it's simple, as I go along my way…
my psalm is written in my heart, as I usually start my day.

By jc

Ode To A Friend

You my friend, my special friend,
Hold a vital part of me…
The part that wants to know you more
My heart, you get for free.
You my friend, my wonderful friend,
Oh how you encourage me so…
I feel renewed, after being with you,
You inspire me deep in my soul.

And now I see you in a whole new light.
A light that I just can't explain.
I fear it's your light, and it's not very bright…
It's dimming from clouds and the rain.
Tell me my friend, my beautiful friend,
What is it that I can do?
The countless times you've encouraged me…
Now I want to encourage you.

Although things may not be perfect my friend.
And this may be redundant to you…
The Lord that lifts up when you share Him with me,
Is the same Lord that helps to lift you.

I will give you my heart and my hand, my dear friend
And this one thing I hope you believe…
It is always nice to Give Hope to a friend
But sometimes you have to receive.

By jc

The Game

You walk around this life, trying to be big sexy,
ghetto-fabulous or cool.
And you say you love Jesus, but your playing the
Devils fool.
Yeah you say the Lord protects you, and He knows
you by name
But realize the Devil knows you too; cause your
playing in the game.

That's right, the Devil has the joystick, when you put
your Jesus down.
You know, those times when you get weak, and you
don't want your Jesus around.
He takes control of your body and mind, he moves so
quick it will blind you.
You'll do the things that Christ saved you from,
cause you left you Christ behind you.

The Devil won't stop at level 1, Cause the devil is in it
to win it.
And you might catch a glimpse of the Love of Christ,
and forget that you were in it.
And hold up, this game aint just for dudes, You
ladies, oh yes you too can play it.
Cause the Devil uses dual controllers, and what
happens next? Let me say it.
Just like in the days of Adam and Eve, like the days
of Sodom and Gomorrah,
The flesh gets weak, and what started out nice, ends
up nasty on the floor–a
Word to the wise, I know this as truth and I pass this
on to you, you see...
If you Love Jesus and you do God, Then you don't
have to do me.

With lies and deceit he plays this game. He can take
this game to another level.

His "power move" is divide and conquer. He's a tough gamer this one the Devil.
Go get that drink, go have your sex, go smoke that blunt, go cut yourself then feel lost.
Cause your flesh won the game this time my friend, but it won it at a cost.

So here's the good news, The games Not done, and you play this till you retire.
Jesus has already won the victory, and the Devil is a liar.
Look, just give Jesus full control; His hand is quick and steady.
The game would be so much easier my friend, haven't you messed it up already?

Jesus is the Master Gamer. And Jesus is the Prize.
Jesus is the One to Save you when you fall for the Devils lies.

By jc

Three Monkeys Ditty

Three Monkeys climbed a tree one day, to see if God was there,
Three monkeys just like you and me, except for all the hair.

One monkey went around the tree with his hands upon his ears.
So when God called him, he didn't move, the monkey didn't hear.

The second Monkey heard it, and he wanted to tell his brothers..
But his hands were over his mouth so he couldn't tell the others.

Now the third monkey heard God, and he had a mouth to tell…
But his eyes were covered by his hands and out the tree he fell.

We know these monkeys as hear no evil, speak no evil and see no evil…
Maybe, it means hear, speak and see no God?

Which monkey are you?

W.W.J.D.?

What would Jesus do? What would Jesus say?
If He would take a note on how we loved these days.
What would Jesus do? What would Jesus say?
What if He knew we took His gift of love and turned it into a cliché'.
Do you think He'd think it strange? Or would He think it great?
That now instead of giving His love, it was now ok to hate.
Hold up now brother, what's this you say? I don't hate people
I'm not that way.
REALLY? OK
Tell me what would Jesus think if He knew how much time you spent,
Finding ways to condemn someone because they practice Lent?
How about your neighbor up the street? Who's black or white or gay?
You treat them different cause they're not "saved like you"
Now what would Jesus say?
We Christians today spend so much time, fitting others into our glove.
What would Jesus do? Oh if only Jesus knew how we changed His definition of love.
Love thy neighbor as thyself. Judge not lest ye be judged.
I didn't think to love like Christ, meant I could carry a grudge.
Now I'm not judging, I'm just praying,
We need to spend less time judging, and more time saying....
I LOVE YOU my brother, I reach out my hand, to help lift you when you fall.
I'll feed you when you're hungry

I'll clothe you when you're naked
I'll answer when you call.
So, here's the answer to the question, we've all been looking for.
You won't find it on the jewelry that you bought down at the store.
The answer my friend, is really the question, put out to me and you.
Can you Love enough to lose your life? Cause that's what Jesus would do.
Jesus died, so that we all may be saved, not just those who know the story.
And if we all did what Jesus would do...
We'd all sing His praises in Glory.

By jc

BOOK FOUR

I Play the Drums… I Aint' Got No Melody

Let's start this one out with a mystery; why would God allow someone to create something they cannot finish? If you have the answer then my dilemma is solved. You see, I play drums, all kinds of drums, some better than others; but none of them will play a lick of a melody. So why, no, how do I write "songs"?
Granted, when I write them I can literally hear the music in my head. By the time it's on paper and edited, it has become a poem, with a chorus and bridge in it. Maybe God has a great sense of humor. Maybe there is a gifted musician/mind reader around the bend. Maybe I need to take piano lessons…NOT!
So now please, take out your instrument of choice, put on your thinking caps and lets make music! Oh, and while you're at it, let your own Joy Come Forth!

jc

Chopstix

I know a lady'
Who just had a baby
and maybe that baby
will never know...

That the father who made it
was sadly related
and although we hate it
it's here.

The world has got to change its heart...
Re arrange its parts ...in this story or...
This child will not be spared the pain
and the story repeats again.

But just like with chopstix, I have to repeat this
But this time its bigger and so we move on to...

How this poor baby
is now a young lady
and while she's out dating
she fills the void of her heart with

some other that acts like her father
and although it's different its clear...

The world has got to change its heart...
Re arrange its parts ...in this story or...
This couples life will be stained...
and the story repeats again.

But just like with chopstix, I have to repeat this
But this time its bigger and so we move on to...

This lady and man
pray for some other plan
They take hold of God's hand
and He leads them into..

A talk with a preacher

Who shows them some teachers
Who gives these new creatures
God's Love...So what happens next is...
this lady
who just had a baby
who's daddy is crazy in love with him.

And they raise him with love
that they learned from above
and the story goes on and on..
Fin.
By jc

Every Day

To you my love...
You shine brighter than all the stars above, and
You bring light into the dark of my life.

And when you speak...
It's oh so soft, and it makes me weak... I
Want nothing more than you by my side.

REFRAIN:
But you are there, and I am here,
And it's hard to fight and hold back the tears... SO

Every day, I ask the Lord if He can find a way to-
Bring us back together for the rest of our days...and then I
pray,
God you know I love her, and I know that this is right,
If I can't love her forever; than just tonight.

To you my girl...
When I look into your eyes I see your world, and
It's beautiful, and that's where I want to be.

And when you smile...
It warms my soul across the miles, and
I die inside, cause you're not here with me.

REFRAIN:
But you are there, and I am here,
And it's hard to fight and hold back the tears….. SO

Every day, I ask the Lord if He can find a way to-
Bring us back together for the rest of our days...and then I
pray,
God you know I love her, and I know that this is right,
If I can't love her forever, than just tonight.

BRIDGE:
My friends keep trying to tell me.
That these things just don't work out
But they don't love you like I do
And I know without a doubt... So...

Every day, I ask the Lord if He can find a way to-
Bring us back together for the rest of our days...and then I
pray,
God you know I love her, and I know that this is right,
If I can't love her forever, than just tonight.

If only I could hold her. One more night.

By jc

Praise The Lord

From the first day of creation…to the dawning of this day
Praise the Lord. All creatures Praise the Lord

From the depth of the oceans… to the desert dry and bare
Praise the Lord. All creatures Praise the Lord

Lift your hands all you elders…and all children far and near
Praise the Lord. All creatures Praise the Lord

Let us sing to Him a new song…to be heard from everywhere
Praise the Lord. All creatures Praise the Lord

Chorus

Praise the Lord all creatures praise the Lord
For He is worthy to be praised
Let His name be exalted, let our hearts to Him proclaim
Praise the Lord all creatures praise the Lord

From the king in his castle…to the beggar on the street
Praise the Lord. All people Praise the Lord

From the top of the mountains to the grass beneath our feet
Praise the Lord. All people Praise the Lord

In our times of plenty, and those time when things look bad
Praise the Lord. All people Praise the Lord

Lift your Hearts and voices, for the Lord will make you glad
Praise the Lord. All people Praise the Lord

Chorus

Praise the Lord all creatures praise the Lord
For He is worthy to be praised
Let His name be exalted, let our hearts to Him proclaim
Praise the Lord all creatures praise the Lord

At the birth of a newborn and the passing of our friends
Praise the Lord. All people Praise the Lord

From the dawn of creation, to the time this world shall end
Praise the Lord. All people Praise the Lord

When our voices grow weary, and our spirits start to doubt
Praise the Lord. All people Praise the Lord

Let the rocks and the grass and the mountains start to shout
Praise the Lord. All people Praise the Lord

Chorus

Praise the Lord all creatures praise the Lord
For He is worthy to be praised
Let His name be exalted, let our hearts to Him proclaim
Praise the Lord all creatures praise the Lord
Halleluiah…Praise the Lord!!

By jc

That Crazy Man

There was a time in my life… not so long ago….
I would do anything… to put on the show
I was living life…or was life living me?

I used to flirt with the ladies… hang out with the guys.
Do anything… that delighted my eyes.
I was doing all right… But that was what I wanted you to see.

(And they'd say)

That boy is crazy, that boy is wild
That boy was like that, since he was a child
That boy has something… that no one can explain…

That boy looks happy, when he's in a crowd
When he's alone in his room, he cries out loud
What he's crying for…can only come from above…
That boy needs love.

There was a time in my life… I remember it well
I was walking a tightrope…between heaven and hell
There was a voice it was calling… calling me by name.

It told me I'll be your savior…I'll set you free
I'll give you all the love…you will ever need
I'll make you different… just fall down on your knees.

(Now they say)

That man is crazy, that man is wild
That man was praying last week with my child
That man has something some folks can't explain

You can tell he's happy…when he's in a crowd
And he loves his Jesus… and he wears him proud
And he shares the gift…he received from above
That man has love.

If any man be in Christ he is a new creation…

And by the love of Christ, we hope for reconciliation
For this whole entire nation…

There was a boy all-alone… in the middle of a crowd
There was a girl who stood silent… in a group so loud
There was a man who could walk… beside them in their pain…

(He tells them)

If you feel locked out, someone holds the key
If your heart feels sick, there is a remedy
His name is Jesus, and he did the same for me…He did the same for me.

That man may be crazy, he may be wild
But that man sees Jesus in the eyes of every child
That man still cries out to his God up above
Please send us love…please send us love.

By jc

The Sequel

Prepare ye the way for the Sequel,
For nothing else can equal; the way the second coming's
going to change your life.

Prepare ye the way for the Master
The day is coming faster
The Holy Spirit's cutting thru just like a knife.

And don't spend the last days wishing,
Cause when people come up missing
You'll be wondering what it is that you can do.

God has a plan for the people
Who keep on living sinful,
The Bible is the word that is instructing you.

So, just give your life to the Savior,
And change the bad behavior,
And then you'll see that Jesus is the only way.

This is the thing that I'm saying,
Never cease from praying
Cause the title of the Sequel is called
JUDGEMENT DAY

By jc

UNTIL YOU

Here I am Lord…broken and tired and bruised.
Here I am Lord…Life full of pain and abuse.
I was lost Lord… I didn't know what I could do
Until You…

Here we stand Lord… a world full of hatred and pain
Here we stand Lord… Were stuck in the storm and the rain
Hear our cry Lord… we don't know how, we can make it thru
Until You…

Until You…
Took the pain to set everyone free
Until You…
Shed your blood and you died just for me
Until You…
Died and buried then raised,
You alone I will praise…
From now on till my journey is through
Until You

Sometimes Lord we stumble, and sometimes Lord we fall…
By your grace Lord were lifted back up.

So till you come again, I will lift up my hands…
I can never praise you enough…

Until You…
Come again and we know not the hour
Until You…
Come again Lord in all of your power
Until You…
Call my name Lord out loud,
I'll meet you in the clouds…Let your mercy Lord pour out on me…
Until You…

By jc

An Ode to The Mothers

This is an ode to the mothers. Whose life I do adore.
To the mothers of the children; that in pain each woman bore.

How beautiful the belly, that so many mothers hide.
The stretch marks are her honor; they are the badges of giving life.

To the mothers that give love, to the mothers that give care.
To the mothers that raise children… when there is no father there.

To the mothers who've had babies, and then given them away.
Be proud that you even had them; they may change the world some day.

To the mothers who were pregnant, whose hearts may now be torn.
Because of the abortion, or your child was never born.

Keep on trying, if you want one. Please stop making them if you don't.
Babies love you when they feel you; they even love you, when you wont…

To the mothers who have babies that they care for after they're grown
And the separation never comes, keep the faith; you're not alone.

Have you ever stopped to wonder? Why the Earth is called a mother?
Like a mom she brings forth life and resource,
And protection like no other.

This one's for the mothers. Who do the best they can,
To turn little girls to women... and turn little boys to men.
I lift my hands to bless you; I send prayers of peace and love.
This tribute to every mother, God's gift, from up above.

By
jc Crawford

THE NEXT PAGES ARE BLANK (if you didn't look ahead already).
An invitation for you to put notes, thoughts or jot down the emergency bible verse you were reminded of.
It's also a place to let your own
JOY COME FORTH!

Thank You & God Bless

jc Crawford

www.ingramcontent.com/pod-product-compliance
Lightning Source LLC
Chambersburg PA
CBHW051715040426
42446CB00008B/895